J977   Crisman, Ruth.
The Mississippi

NEWHALL 104

8⁹⁰

THE
MISSISSIPPI

THE
MISSISSIPPI

BY RUTH CRISMAN

FRANKLIN WATTS
New York | London | Toronto | Sydney
1984 | A FIRST BOOK

The author wishes to extend thanks to

the U.S. Army Corps of Engineers;
the U.S. Coast Guard;
Wisconsin Department of Natural Resources;
Mud Island Mississippi River Museum;
Twin City Barge, Inc., *Delta Queen;*
American Commercial Barge Line Co.

Map by Vantage Art, Inc.

Cover photograph courtesy of
the author

Photographs courtesy of:
Wisconsin State Department of Natural Resources: pp. 5, 53;
Missouri Department of Agriculture: p. 9
The Bettmann Archive: pp. 13, 16, 27;
Ewing Galloway: p. 21; Ruth Crisman: pp. 30, 60;
Mississippi River Commission, Corps of Engineers: p. 37;
United Nations/Army Corps of Engineers: p. 44.

Library of Congress Cataloging in Publication Data

Crisman, Ruth.
The Mississippi.

(A First book)
Includes index.
Summary: Describes the Mississippi River and its effect
on the geography, history, economy, and people of the
region through which it flows. Also discusses some of the
special problems of this waterway and its future prospects.
1. Mississippi River—Juvenile literature.
2. Mississippi River Valley—Juvenile literature.
[1. Mississippi River. 2. Mississippi River Valley.
3. Rivers] I. Title.

F351.C74   1984   977   84-7233
ISBN 0-531-04826-8

CONTENTS

TO YOUNG PEOPLE
EVERYWHERE:

TO DISCOVER, ENJOY,
AND PROTECT
OUR GREATEST RIVER

CHAPTER ONE

THE WANDERING MISSISSIPPI

It is the longest river in the world—
four thousand three hundred miles . . .
It is also the crookedest river in the world,
since in one part of its journey it uses up
one thousand three hundred miles to cover
the same ground that the crow would fly over
in six hundred and seventy-five.

Life on the Mississippi (1883)
Mark Twain

The mighty Mississippi has been shaped by many forces of nature. One of the worst earthquakes in our history caused the Mississippi River to overflow its banks at New Madrid, Missouri, on December 16, 1811. Great waves churned the river's bed. Huge chunks of land slid down bluffs and hillsides. Some areas were pushed up, and larger areas sank as much as 25 feet (7.5 m). Thousands of trees were swept into the raging waters. Sand bars and islands disappeared. The terrible force of water moved downriver, reversed course, and turned back on itself. The Mississippi River ran backward!

The river floods and earthquakes forced the settlers to move back to safety several times. Many people were killed. It was felt over an area of almost a million square miles, from Canada to Louisiana. The crazy river had created Reelfoot Lake, Tennessee, where no lake had been before!

As a result, Congress passed laws to protect the land from river floods. The United States Army Corps of Engineers constructed locks and dams on the Upper River between St. Paul, Minnesota, and St. Louis, Missouri. The organization also improved the navigation channel of the Lower River and protected its banks from flooding with dikes and levees of concrete, stone, and dirt. Levees and floodwalls guard both sides of the Mississippi and its tributaries for nearly three times the length of the Great Wall of China. People try to control the river and use it for their purposes, but they always face the danger of floods.

For convenience, the Army Corps of Engineers divides the river into three sections. The Upper River flows from St. Paul to St. Louis, the Middle River flows 200 miles (320 km) from the mouth of the Missouri to the mouth of the Ohio, and the Lower River flows from Cairo, Illinois, to the Gulf of Mexico. However, today the term Middle River is not often used.

The Mississippi River and its tributary rivers drain 41 percent of our nation's water from all or part of thirty-one states and two Canadian provinces. Its 250 tributaries and branches comprise the third largest drainage basin in the world. The tributaries

gather excess rainfall and the overflow of springs and lakes and pour their waters into the Mississippi. An average of 350 billion gallons (1,325 billion liters) of water return to the sea each day. This longest river in North America drains 1¼ million square miles (3,237,000 sq km) of land or about one eighth of the entire area of the continent. More than one third of the nation's population live and work in the region.

Where is the Mississippi River? In the United States, two long mountain chains, the Appalachians in the East and the Rocky Mountains, the largest mountain chain in the West, form a huge valley. Down this valley flows the Mississippi River with fifty-seven navigable rivers contributing to its waters.

On a map the Mississippi River resembles a giant tree. The two largest branches are the Ohio and the Missouri. As it flows along, the river forms at least part of the boundary line of ten mid-American states. Wisconsin, Illinois, Kentucky, Tennessee, and Mississippi touch the east sides. On the west are located Minnesota, Iowa, Missouri, Arkansas, and Louisiana. The Mississippi wriggles and twists its way south to plant roots in the Gulf of Mexico.

The Mississippi River is the main stem of a network of inland waterways, a system 12,350 miles (19,760 km) in length which includes the Ohio, Missouri, Illinois, and Tennessee rivers.

The river's wandering course cuts across low banks and loops, and bends around islands, changing its length. The width of the Mississippi River also varies from a few feet to more than a mile. The river tends to widen at shallow places and to become narrow at deep ones. At its source at Lake Itasca, Minnesota, it is possible to wade across the river. At St. Louis, it's almost a mile wide. From New Orleans to the Gulf of Mexico, it narrows down to less than 1,000 feet (300 m).

If you stepped in the Mississippi River, how deep would it be? It depends on whether you are in the river at St. Paul or New Orleans. It is shallow as you canoe the river lakes of the Itasca State Park area. From St. Paul, Minnesota, to Cairo, Illinois, the Army Corps of Engineers maintains a 9-foot (2.7-m) depth. On

*The Mississippi River and backwaters
near La Crosse, Wisconsin*

the Lower River, the deepest part lies 40 to 100 feet (12 to 30 m) down. Some places are gouged out 200 feet (60 m) deep where the river bends, as deep as a twenty-story building!

The river is constantly building sandbars and washing them away again. Today, the Mississippi River winds through an ancient bed of sand, silt, and mud made thousands of years ago. On the bottom lie fossil skulls of mastodons from the glacial past, when prehistoric elephants roamed America.

Where did the sediment on the river's bottom come from? Millions of years ago during the Ice Age, huge mountains of ice covered most of the North American continent. At the end of the Ice Age, twelve thousand years ago, the earth's climate became warmer. The glaciers melted. Ice pushed and scraped, grinding up boulders into flourlike silt, grains of rock, and clay. The action of the ice changed the shape of the land. The immense runoff of melted snow carried the silt and sand down the Mississippi trench, partly filling its depths.

When the glaciers retreated, Minnesota became a "land of ten thousand lakes." One of these lakes, the source of the Mississippi River, had been a mystery for a long time. Many explorers searched for the headwaters. In 1832, Chippewa Indians guided Henry Schoolcraft to the lake they called Lake Omoskos Sogiagon, "Elk Lake." The lake divides into three branches, long and thin like antlers. Water flows in three directions—north to Hudson Bay, Canada, east to Lake Superior, and south to the Mississippi River. Schoolcraft raised an American flag, fired a round of shots, and named the lake *Itasca.* He created the name by joining three syllables from two Latin words, *veritas caput,* which means "true head." Today, however, many geologists believe that glacial lakes supply the headwaters.

Each year thousands of people visit the headwaters and enjoy the beauty of Itasca State Park. The park encloses a hundred lakes, springs, and creeks. It is mostly a wilderness area where people camp, fish, swim, and boat. Woodland birds live in pine, cedar, and spruce trees. From late March to early August, it is possible to look over the lake and see the American Bald Eagle fly to its nesting site.

At Lake Itasca people cross the Mississippi on stepping stones or by wading across it! This clear little stream, less than a foot (.3 m) deep and about 18 feet (5.4 m) across, begins a long, crooked journey south to empty into the Gulf of Mexico, 2,340 miles (3,744 km) away.

To follow that winding Mississippi, the trip begins by canoe, turning past banks where Chippewa Indians and descendants of Scandinavian settlers live. The river loops and bends like a fish-hook north from Lake Itasca to Lake Bemidji, then east, stringing together a chain of lakes. It is necessary to paddle beside streams and ponds, near homes of muskrat, beaver, otter, and mink. Marshlands are filled with wild rice and celery. After 180 miles (289 km), the river turns south near Grand Rapids, Minnesota. It tumbles through small rapids past steep, rising cliffs. The river drops more than 700 feet (210 m) in 513 miles (821 km) from its source to reach the Falls of St. Anthony. By then, it's wide, fast, and sometimes dangerous.

Towboats and pleasure craft pass through the upper and lower locks of the 75-foot (22.5-m) -high Falls. The upper lock is the highest of all the locks on the Upper Mississippi and raises and lowers boats by 50 feet (15 m). In the late 1800s, the Falls produced power for the flour mills, graneries, and lumber companies in the Minneapolis/St. Paul area. Today, the St. Anthony Falls Hydraulic Laboratory, part of the University of Minnesota, overlooks the Falls. The laboratory diverts water at the 50-foot (15-m) level, uses it for research purposes, and releases it to the river below the Falls. At this point, navigation starts for the larger towboats with their heavy barges of petroleum, fertilizer, coal, and grain.

Beginning at St. Anthony Falls, the Upper Mississippi River is controlled by twenty-nine locks and dams, like a descending staircase of water. From below St. Louis to the sea, the river is free of locks and dams.

Many interesting towns such as Wabasha, Minnesota; Prairie du Chien, Wisconsin; Keokuk, Iowa; Rock Island, Illinois; and Hannibal, Missouri are located along the Upper River. For almost 1,000 miles (1,600 km) the river runs by bluffs, rolling hills, and small islands, inviting places for campers. As the Mississippi flows south, it is fed by lesser tributaries—the St. Croix, Wisconsin, Des Moines, and Illinois rivers. After traveling 1,215 miles (1,944 km) from its source, it joins the Missouri River 17 miles (27.2 km) north of St. Louis.

The wide Missouri River, nicknamed "Big Muddy," empties its brown waters into the Mississippi. The clearer Mississippi waters flow side by side with the muddy Missouri for about 100 miles (160 km) before the rivers unite. The Missouri River is the Mississippi's longest tributary. (However, the length of the Mississippi is measured from its headwaters in Lake Itasca, because explorers went to the Upper River region first.)

River markers show the number of miles along the way. The Upper Mississippi begins at mile 0.0 at the mouth of the Ohio River and ends at mile 839.0 at St. Paul. The Lower Mississippi begins at Mile 0.0 at the Head of Passes, near the Gulf of Mexico, and ends at mile 955.8 at Cairo, Illinois.

At the small town of Cairo, the Ohio flows into the Mississippi. This second largest tributary carries more water from its larger river branches—the Cumberland, Tennessee, and Wabash—than the Missouri or the Mississippi!

The Lower Mississippi River begins at Cairo and empties into the Gulf of Mexico, about 1,000 miles (1,600 km) away. Between Memphis and New Orleans, it collects the waters from the St. Francis, Arkansas, and White rivers. Then past Natchez, Mississippi, the Ouachita and Red rivers add their streams in central Louisiana.

The Alluvial Valley of the Lower Mississippi begins just below Cape Girardeau, Missouri. The alluvial deposits are clay, silt,

*The muddy Missouri River empties into the Mississippi
a few miles above St. Louis.*

sand, and gravel material left by the river flooding the land during periods of high water. It covers 35,000 square miles (56,000 sq km) in parts of seven states. Shaped like a funnel, the valley is 30 to 125 miles (48 to 200 km) wide and 600 miles (960 km) long. Dikes and levees protect the riverbanks so that people can occupy the land.

The Mississippi River enters the narrowest part of the Alluvial Valley 90 miles (144 km) south of New Orleans at the Gulf of Mexico. It enters through a vast delta, which is the alluvial deposit at the river's mouth. Its roots spread out at the Head of Passes (North, South, and Southwest) where the Mississippi River ends its journey to the sea.

Sometimes a fog covers the river. Whistle sounds are heard from passing boats. River work goes on as usual, by means of radar and marine telephone. The long, low tows of barges push on silently with their cargoes. Searchlights pierce the darkness. Boats follow the floating markers that glow red and green to mark the channel. The smaller craft tie up for the night, waiting for the weather to clear.

In the morning light, people go about their business again. They work, live, and play on the river. And it all began long ago.

CHAPTER TWO

THE DISCOVERED RIVER

Joy to thee, my brave canoe,—
There's no wing so swift as you;
Right and left the bubbles rise—
Right and left the pine wood flies;
Birds and clouds and tide and wind
We shall leave ye all behind.
Joy to thee, my brave canoe,—
There's no wing so swift as you.
Joy to thee, my brave canoe,—
There's no wing so swift as you.

Voyageur's Song
French Canadian Folk Tune

For many years the river was unexplored. The Algonquin-speaking woodland tribes lived around the lower Great Lakes. They hunted bear and deer, gathered wild fruit and berries, and grew maize and rice. The Indians paddled their canoes down the *Missi Sipi,* the Algonquin name for "Big Waters" or "Great River."

Columbus discovered the New World when he was looking for a water route to India. No one knows for sure, but he may have been the first European to see the mouth of the Mississippi River at the Gulf of Mexico.

In 1539, after his plunder and conquest of Peru, Spanish explorer Hernando de Soto dreamed of finding more gold. He and his Conquistadores claimed Florida for Spain. They fought large numbers of Indians and explored much of the area that later became our Southern states. On May 21, 1541, de Soto discovered the Mississippi River south of what is now Memphis. He called it *Rio del Espiritu Santo,* "the River of the Holy Spirit." On the bluffs above the river stood the thatched-roofed houses and burial grounds of the Chickasaws. De Soto fought off Indians, built boats and barges, and crossed the river.

The Conquistadores pushed into present day Arkansas and Louisiana. Each time de Soto captured Indians, they told him the gold was farther west with the next tribe. After ten years of searching, de Soto found no gold. He died of fever. A few Spanish soldiers hid his body from the Indians in the Mississippi, then made their way back to Mexico.

One hundred and thirty-two years later, France sent Louis Joliet, mapmaker and fur trader, to search for a water route to the Orient. Joliet set out from Quebec with Jacques Marquette, a Jesuit missionary, in birch-bark canoes, *pirogues.* With the help of French canoemen *voyageurs* and friendly Indians, they traveled by way of the Fox and Wisconsin rivers, and down the Mississippi as far as the mouth of the Arkansas River. They met the Quapaws, the Indian name for "downstream people," who told them the Mississippi flowed into the Gulf of Mexico. When the Quapaws showed them trinkets from the Spaniards, the French

*French explorers Louis Joliet and Jacques Marquette
traveled down the Mississippi as far as the mouth of
the Arkansas River in the early 1670s.*

feared they would be captured and decided to return to Canada. They were convinced that the Mississippi River emptied into the Gulf and did not cut through to the Pacific Ocean.

The French settled along the Upper Mississippi first, claiming the territory for France. It was easier to establish forts and trading posts close to Canada. They carried on a profitable business with the Indians, trading for valuable furs and selling them in Canada and France.

When Robert de La Salle heard about the river, he was eager to conquer more lands in America for France. He believed the Mississippi was one of the great rivers on earth. La Salle's expedition canoed down the Mississippi where Jolliet and Marquette had gone, down past the Arkansas River to the Gulf of Mexico. He met hostile Indians, yet managed to trade with them for needed supplies.

When he came to the place where the river divided into three parts, La Salle planted the Standard of Royal France in the sand at the river's mouth. In April 1682, he claimed all the Mississippi River, all the branches and tributaries, as well as "nations, peoples, provinces, towns, villages, mines, minerals . . . for King Louis the Great." In the King's honor, he named this place *Louisiana.*

France did nothing with La Salle's Louisiana. In 1763 Louis XV granted the lands to Spain. After the Revolutionary War, American colonists occupied English lands and began settling in Spanish territory. In 1801, Napoleon threatened Spain with war over Louisiana. Spain gave the Louisiana "headache" back to France. Two years later, in 1803, the United States bought the Louisiana Territory—and the Mississippi River that went with it—from France for four cents an acre.

After the Louisiana Purchase, President Jefferson sent Meriwether Lewis and William Clark to explore the Purchase land between the Mississippi River and the Rocky Mountains. They explored the Missouri River from its mouth at the Mississippi to its source in Montana. They crossed the Continental Divide and reached the Pacific Ocean by way of the Snake and Columbia

Rivers. The expedition opened a rich new land for the United States.

In 1809, the Ohio and Mississippi Valley areas were still considered the West. As people followed the river tributaries to the Mississippi, they settled the land with ax and oxen. They cut down trees to plant corn and wheat. Some people farmed land. Others became rivermen. Log rafts measured the length of three city blocks. Professional boatmen were hired who knew how to deliver valuable cargo downriver. Abraham Lincoln hired himself out on two such trips. On a flatboat he delivered produce more than 1,000 miles (1,600 km) down the Ohio and Mississippi to New Orleans.

Farmers loaded their one-way boats and drifted all the way to New Orleans. They sold their grain and lumber from the flatboat there. The problem was how to get home. If they walked or rode northeast into the Ohio Valley on the Natchez Trace, robbers and cutthroats were waiting. If they could afford it, farmers rode on keelboats or worked their way back. Twenty people could sail, paddle, or pole the keelboat upstream, or, hitched to a rope, pull it from ashore.

People said that it puffed like a teakettle and would never work, but in 1811 the first steamboat navigated down the Ohio and Mississippi rivers. The *New Orleans*, with a deep, round hull, was designed by Robert Fulton and built in Pittsburgh, Pennsylvania. It carried freight on its lower level and people upstairs.

At Wheeling, West Virginia, Henry Shreve, an ex-flatboat captain, built the steamboat *Washington.* Shreve's new design, a flat shallow hull, sailed on the river instead of in it. The paddle-wheel lay farther back, a "double decker" ugly duckling. The *Washington* was the first steamboat to navigate round trip from Pittsburgh to New Orleans.

In 1817 a canal was proposed to run from Buffalo, New York, on the eastern shore of Lake Erie, to Albany, New York, on the Upper Hudson, passing through the gap in the mountains in the Mohawk Valley region. When the Erie Canal opened in 1825, it

This Currier and Ives engraving shows the variety of river
traffic on the Mississippi in the nineteenth century.

provided a waterway for western expansion. It linked the Great Lakes with the Atlantic Ocean via New York City and the Hudson River.

Settlers moved west into Michigan, Ohio, Indiana, and Illinois. They shipped eastward over the canal or southward down the Ohio and the Mississippi to New Orleans. The Erie Canal cut travel time one third and shipping costs by nine tenths. It opened the Great Lakes area.

It was cheaper to send freight to the East Coast by way of the Mississippi, and the long sea passage, than one tenth the distance over the Appalachians. Freight company profits were high, but terrible disasters left many steamboats at the bottom of the river. The river was full of snags and sandbars. There was always the danger of exploding boilers and collisions.

In 1835–36 more than 1,200 steamboats unloaded their cargoes in New Orleans. The freight received amounted to more than 437,000 tons (396,359 tonnes). As late as 1840, one fifth of the freight handled on the Lower Mississippi was by flatboats, keelboats, and barges. Between 1830 and 1840, "the Golden Age of River Traffic," New Orleans became the leading export city of the United States and one of the leading ports of the world.

During those golden years showy packet boats carried passengers upstairs and cargo downstairs. On the outside of the wooden steamboat, decorations were cut in fanciful shapes that looked like frosted gingerbread. Inside, river gamblers used marked cards to win hard-earned dollars from unsuspecting farmers.

In 1827 the Baltimore and Ohio became the first railroad to carry freight and passengers. By 1840 there were 2,800 miles (4,480 km) of track, most of it parallel to the Mississippi. For the first time, farmers, manufacturers, and merchants had overland transportation that moved large volumes of goods and people. Some types of factories no longer needed to be located on the river. Boat landings that used to handle river traffic were vacant. Sawmills and warehouses were empty. The sounds of "steamboat a-comin' " were gone.

By the 1850s the North and South were bitterly divided over the problem of slavery. The Civil War broke out in 1861. One of the most vital battles was fought at Vicksburg in 1863. After a forty-seven-day siege by armored vessels and the Union Army, the Confederate forces surrendered. There was enormous loss of lives on both sides. The North opened the Mississippi River all the way to the sea and blocked off supply lines for the Southern states. Control of the Mississippi played a major part in the Union victory.

After the Civil War, however, steamboats returned to the river. Now they were faster, bigger, and more ornate than ever. The *Natchez* and the *Robert E. Lee* held a famous race from New Orleans to St. Louis in 1870, and the *Robert E. Lee* won in 3 days, 18 hours, and 14 minutes. In order to win, the crew stripped off unnecessary wooden structure and took on extra fuel supplies while steaming full speed upstream.

Today the paddlewheelers *Delta Queen* and *Mississippi Queen* represent the only overnight passenger steamboats in operation on the Ohio and Mississippi Rivers. They race each year from New Orleans to St. Louis. Usually the *Delta Queen* cruise takes thirteen days to get from New Orleans to Cincinnati, Ohio.

As the railroads grew, providing east-west transportation, commercial traffic dwindled on the river. During World War I, the U.S. Government created the Federal Barge Lines. The War Department, in its desperate need to move goods, revived stern-wheelers and barges. Soon stern-wheelers pushed bargeloads of cargo up and down river. The Federal Barge Lines still operate today under private ownership.

World War I produced a major change in river trade. Shipping increased. In 1929, diesel- and gasoline-powered towboats moved cargoes of grain, coal, oil, iron, steel, sulfur, and limestone. Today there are over 1,800 barge and towing companies in business. They deliver more than 580 million tons (526 million tonnes) of cargo each year on the Mississippi River System.

CHAPTER THREE

THE WORKING MISSISSIPPI

Have you heard about Paul Bunyan
and his sky-blue ox Big Babe?
Paul Bunyan and Big Babe plowed
this ditch of the Mississippi
a thousand miles from Minneapolis
to the Ohio River.
The hills are just clods turned up
by Paul's monstrous plow!

Lumberjack Yarn from
A Treasury of American Folklore

The Mississippi River looks quite different today from the way it did in the early 1800s, when it was free to change course as it pleased. The force of the river's current caved in banks of soft, erodible soil. This caused the river to flow in a series of wide bends. People might find the river a mile away, at their door-steps, or on top of their houses.

Congress realized that control of the Mississippi was neces-sary for the growth and protection of people in the Mississippi Valley and for westward expansion. It passed laws which gave to the Army Corps of Engineers the task of keeping the waterways open and increasing their usefulness.

In 1879, Congress created the Mississippi River Commission, which still functions. Its tasks were to find ways to improve the river's channel for navigation, protect the river from caving banks, prevent floods, and promote commerce. This began a new era for the people of the Mississippi Valley.

The Corps of Engineers surveyed the Mississippi River's course. They cleaned out snags and sandbars, dredged the river bottom, and protected sides of river banks. The Engineers con-structed locks and dams on the Ohio River.

In 1922, Congress appropriated $42 million for navigation and flood control. Lawmakers recognized the need to create a permanent shipping channel from New Orleans to Minneapolis/ St. Paul on the Mississippi, and from Pittsburgh to Cairo on the Ohio.

By 1940 the Army Corps of Engineers had constructed twen-ty-nine locks and dams on the Upper Mississippi River, some with auxiliary channels. From the first lock at the Falls of St. Anthony to the last lock above St. Louis the river falls about 420 feet (126 m) in a distance of 669 miles (1,070 km). The Engineers maintained the navigation channel at a minimum 9-ft. (2.7-m) depth and 400-ft. (120-m) width. Towboats and recreation traffic can navigate the Upper River now in times of low water.

Waters from the Minnesota, St. Croix, Wisconsin, Rock, Tur-key, Maquoketa, Wapsipinicon, Cedar, Iowa, Des Moines, and

*Government Dam and Lock #1 near Minneapolis/St. Paul
is the first of twenty-nine locks built by
the Army Corps of Engineers on the Upper Mississippi.*

the Illinois rivers, as well as smaller streams, flow into the Mississippi between Minneapolis and St. Louis. During the winter, the Upper Mississippi River, the Missouri, and the Ohio are normally closed by ice. On the lakes and rivers, "ice fishing" is very popular. People rent heated fish houses and place them on the frozen river. Four or five people go inside and fish through a hole cut in the ice.

In the spring towboats and barges begin service again. When the ice breaks up, it becomes a danger to water traffic. Many times huge chunks of ice are pushed through the locks just like a boat!

Often heavy rains wash topsoil from farmers' fields. The snow melts and sends down water, flooding the streams and scouring the riverbank. If dredging isn't done, the soil, sand, and sediment will fill the river to a depth of less than 9 feet (2.7 m). Dredging deepens and widens the river channel and keeps it at a proper depth for boats. The dredged underwater material is pumped through vacuum pipelines to shore or removed on barges to a disposal site.

The Corps of Engineers, the U.S. Fish and Wildlife Service, and the Environmental Protection Agency study the problems of cost, removal, and dump sites. These important decisions affect people and the animal-plant environment.

On the Mississippi River System the U.S. Coast Guard looks after boating safety, search and rescue, and provides aids to navigation. It inspects vessels and issues licenses to boat operators. Search and rescue teams launch boats and patrol planes within minutes of calls to rescue survivors from disasters. They even save oil-soaked birds! LORAN Stations, Long Range Aids to Navigation, emit radio signals that locate a ship's position within a few yards.

From time to time the Coast Guard checks the positions of the red and green buoys that mark the navigation channel. Accidents happen when buoys are thrown off course by a passing boat or by a changing river current.

All riverboat captains must stay between the buoys marking the channel. They communicate by marine radio with their offices miles away, their crews on the tows, and other boats on the river. Pilots agree by signal how to pass each other.

The modern towboat found on the inland waterways does not use a spoked wheel in the pilothouse. Today's pilots drive diesel engines with hydraulic steering and read their positions on radar and depth finders.

On the Upper River, towboats average fifteen barges apiece. Each barge holds up to 1,500 tons (1,361 tonnes) of cargo. It would take sixty semi-trucks or fifteen rail cars to carry the same amount of tonnage! Millions of dollars worth of barges and tows work the river. From their pilothouses, five stories above the water, the pilots look across the towboats, a distance sometimes longer than three football fields.

Annual traffic on the river has more than doubled in the last ten years. Barge tows catch up with each other and must wait in line, sometimes as long as eight hours, to enter locks. Major barge traffic navigates the Mississippi or Illinois rivers. The Illinois Waterway is a connecting link between the Great Lakes, the St. Lawrence Seaway, and the Mississippi River.

You are welcome to "boat watch" at an Army Corps viewing area as the tows go through the locks. The locks and dams form a series of lakes called "pools," a fairly flat stretch of river contained by the navigation dam. The boat enters the lock, a rectangular-shaped chamber made of concrete, with steel gates at either end. The lock gates are the elevator doors. The water surface in the lock chamber is the floor. The lock fills and empties by gravity, which forces the water to seek its own level. No power is used except for the machinery that controls the valves and gates. The lock takes a boat safely and quickly from one water level to another.

Usually there are corn, wheat, and soybeans going downriver, and coal, molasses, and petroleum products headed upriver. According to the Army Corps of Engineers, 60 percent of barge cargo consists of petroleum products and coal. Building materials are next, followed by grain, chemicals, and then iron and steel products. Barge traffic in the United States now totals more than 1 billion tons (907,000,000 tonnes) annually.

Crops move by truck and rail to river terminals for their journey by water. A typical grain tow bound downriver from Minneapolis/St. Paul will transit twenty-seven locks before reaching St. Louis. From there it is another 1,027 miles (1643.2 km) to New Orleans. The river is wide and the grain convoys swell to as many as forty or more barges nearly a quarter of a mile long. Farmers store their grain in silos at different locations, from where it can be loaded on hopper barges. The tows carry the grain to larger elevators or export ships along the river.

CHAPTER FOUR

MARK TWAIN'S RIVER

Only way to become a pilot
is to learn the river by heart,
like you know your ABC's.
Shape of the river's the whole thing.
It never looks the same, you see.
It's four different rivers—
day, night, up, and downstream.

> Captain Bixby instructs
> young Sam Clemens
> *Life on the Mississippi*

Where the Upper Mississippi flows between St. Paul and St. Louis, attractive groups of houses and boat landings dot the shore. Some towns sit on higher cliffs or rolling hills, others on agricultural plains. People in speedboats and fishing boats stay away from the passing tows as they enjoy the river or picnic on forested islands.

Downriver past Quincy, Illinois, 100 miles (160 km) north of St. Louis, is the 6-square-mile (15.54-sq-km) town of Hannibal, Missouri, "where Mark Twain lives again." A few blocks up from the cobblestone levee, Hannibal is filled with residents and tourists who celebrate the memory of Hannibal's favorite son. Schoolchildren on field trips visit Mark Twain's boyhood home and museum, the Becky Thatcher house, and the Haunted House on Hill Street. High on the bluffs at Riverview Park, a statue of Mark Twain overlooks the river he loved, 300 feet (90 m) below.

Samuel Langhorne Clemens (1835–1910) chose the name Mark Twain from his piloting days. When the leadsman took soundings from the bow of the steamboat, he would call out "M-A-A-A-R-K T-W-A-A-I-N" to the steersman. Mark Twain means "2 fathoms deep" (12 feet or 3.6 m). It also means "safe water ahead." As a riverboat pilot, Sam Clemens had to write and remember every twist and turn, every island and town.

Mark Twain became a newspaperman, a writer, and a lecturer. He wrote stories about his adventures as a boy in Hannibal. Becky Thatcher, Aunt Polly, Huck Finn, and Tom Sawyer were based on people he really knew. Mark Twain's Mississippi filled him with the desire to explore its forested islands, rippling currents, and graceful bends, and in *Huckleberry Finn*, Mark Twain described his adventures on the river.

Showboats brought culture and entertainment to Hannibal and other towns along the Ohio, the Mississippi, and the Illinois rivers and tributaries. The earliest showboats were family-owned. They ventured into regions where churches, newspapers, schools, and theaters had not gone. There was no TV or

Showboats like the Floating Palace *brought entertainment to far-flung river towns.*

radio. But there were Eugene Robinson's Floating Palaces—a museum, menagerie, aquarium, and grand opera house on barges towed by steamboats!

After the Civil War, showboats specialized in vaudeville and melodrama. The sounds of Dixie came to the Upper River from New Orleans. You could hear the banjos playing Stephen Foster songs such as "Oh! Susannah" on the riverboat. As a young boy in Pittsburgh, Foster wrote songs inspired by the work chants of slaves and by romantic tunes of the day. In 1851 he wrote one of his most famous songs, "Old Folks at Home," also known as "Swanee River."

Another musical sound that could be heard five miles away was the call of the steamboat calliope. The calliope had pipes, hooked up to steam, that whistled. Up and down the river people gathered to hear the "whooper" steam piano play. Boats called by such names as *Cotton Blossom, Majestic,* and *Water Queen* brought plays and comedies to every river from the narrow Monongahela in the northeast to the bayous in the South.

To show what life was like on the Mississippi, artists drew maps and scenic pictures. Nathaniel Currier and James Ives, lithographers, sold prints that showed the sports, disasters, natural scenes, and historical events of nineteenth-century life. Prints such as *A Midnight Race on the Mississippi* sold for anywhere from five cents to three dollars.

One hundred and thirteen miles (180.8 km) from Hannibal, just above St. Louis, the Mississippi meets the Missouri River. The "Big Muddy" brings a great number of silt particles suspended in its waters. It carries 275,000 tons (249.425 tonnes) of soil past Omaha, Nebraska, on a given day. It is the longest river in the United States—2,565 miles (4,130 km)—and the Mississippi River's major tributary.

The Missouri River begins in the Rocky Mountain area of southwestern Montana at the confluence of the Jefferson, Madison, and Gallatin rivers. Starting out as a small stream, it meanders through canyons and flows across hundreds of miles of prairies. The river twists east across Montana, south through the Dakotas, and widens to become a boundary between Nebraska and Iowa.

It is joined by its tributaries—the Yellowstone River close to the North Dakota border and the Platte River near Omaha, Nebraska. At Kansas City, Kansas, the river turns east again, flowing past Jefferson City, the state capital of Missouri, to its mouth at the Mississippi River.

Today more than one hundred dams and reservoirs help prevent floods, irrigate lands, and provide electric power for the Missouri River Basin. Missourians enjoy man-made lakes behind the dams, such as Lake of the Ozarks, and Truman and Stockton reservoirs. Near Fort Peck Dam, in Montana, families cruise in small boats or paddle in canoes or on inner tubes.

Kansas City, Missouri, once a fur-trading post, now markets and ships agricultural and metal products, as well as clothing. The Army Corps of Engineers dredged the channel and stabilized the river banks to maintain navigation between Sioux City, Iowa, and St. Louis. However, the speed of the river current increased, and a great deal of government time and money is spent on rock to keep the river in place. The Mississippi River supports twenty times as much barge traffic as the Missouri!

In 1763 a Frenchman named Pierre Laclède sailed up the Mississippi from New Orleans looking for a site to build a fur-trading post. He found a place he liked with high banks, hills, and walnut trees. When you climb the fifty-six steps of the levee to Riverside Park in St. Louis, you'll see that Laclède's settlement has become a modern city. Yet St. Louis still boasts many historical places.

Many kinds of riverboats, showboat restaurants, and museums are located along the waterfront. The fully restored authentic steamboat *Delta Queen*, or a new overnight passenger steamboat, the *Mississippi Queen*, or Jacques Cousteau's *Calypso* may be moored at the river's banks or wharves.

At the entrance to the harbor at St. Louis is the Eads Bridge, which spans the Mississippi. James B. Eads recovered cargoes and wrecks of river steamers with a salvage boat he invented. However, Eads is better known as the engineer and designer of the triple-arch steel bridge named in his honor.

Dedicated on July 4, 1874, after seven years of construction, the 6,220-foot (1,866-m) Eads Bridge connects the states of Illinois and Missouri. It is now a registered national landmark, the first of many bridges built on the Mississippi.

At the Harbor the remarkable Gateway Arch, striking in outline, dominates the waterfront. Built in 1965, it symbolizes the spirit of St. Louis, Gateway City to the West. The Arch stands on the original village plot laid out by Pierre Laclède. A large museum beneath the Arch contains the history of westward expansion, part of the Jefferson National Expansion Memorial.

Designed by Finnish-born architect Eero Saarinen, the Gateway Arch is the tallest national monument, 630 feet (190 m) of stainless steel! A trainlike vehicle runs on special tracks up the hollow curving legs of the Arch. This capsule transporter holds five passengers and in four minutes whisks visitors to the top. There is a breathtaking 30-mile (48-km) view from thirty-two windows on either side of the observation room.

The city of St. Louis is a major transportation center, close to the Ohio, Missouri, and other river approaches. Once grain and furs from St. Louis went down the Mississippi on flatboats. Now tows, loaded with as much as 50,000 tons (45,350 tonnes), leave the harbor daily carrying domestic and foreign freight. Coal comes from Wyoming and Montana to St. Louis by train and is transferred to barges there. It's one of the nation's busiest inland river ports, with large markets for livestock, grain, wool, and lumber. Industries there also ship metals, chemicals, and textiles.

The Gateway Arch in St. Louis

CHAPTER FIVE

THE POWERFUL MISSISSIPPI

I'm a movin', getting under way
Today's a new day, no time to play
I move fast, I move slow
Got many miles to go, before tomorrow
There's a piece of steel for
a man down in Vicksburg
A load of coal that's bound
for Tennessee
A belly full of grain fresh
out of Kansas
And some sweet, sweet sugar
from a land across the sea.
Well, I'm a movin', Yes, I'm a movin' . . .

Song from film
Return to the Sea
(U.S. Army Corps of Engineers)

From St. Louis the mighty Mississippi River drops an average of about 4 inches (10 cm) a mile on its way to the Gulf of Mexico. At the tip of a narrow peninsula near the small town of Cairo, Illinois, the Ohio River drains into the Mississippi. Twenty-five million people live and work in 204,000 square miles (528,360 sq km) of the Ohio Basin.

The Ohio River runs downstream for 975 miles (1,570 km) and lowers by more than 400 feet (120 m). It flows past woodlands, rolling hills, and scenic plains. The river provides water for electric power and steel-making plants, and also irrigates farms of soybeans, tobacco, and corn.

The source of the Ohio is located at the junction of the Allegheny and Monongahela rivers at Pittsburgh, Pennsylvania. A beautiful 200-foot (60-m) -high fountain of water at Point State Park marks the place where the rivers come together, called the Golden Triangle. Pittsburgh set an example for other industrial cities by cleaning up the soot and dirt from its coal-burning furnaces. Now it is a clean, modern city with headquarters for many large manufacturers.

In 1811 the Ohio ran like a torrent during spring floods, but dried into a small stream in the summer heat. In 1870 the Army Corps began a continuing program to build locks and dams on the Ohio to improve navigation and prevent floods. Today the Corps operates twenty locks and dams, making possible a minimum channel depth of 9 feet (2.7 m) and width of 300 feet (90 m).

Bargeloads of coal, petroleum, and grain move downriver past West Virginia, Kentucky, Pennsylvania, Ohio, Indiana, and Illinois. With the increase in shipping, a 1,200-ft (360-m) tow and barges on the Mississippi or Ohio must uncouple and go through the 600-ft (180-m) locks in two sections. At the present time three 1,200-ft (360-m) locks operate on the Ohio River.

Eleven miles (17.6 km) past the Cumberland River at Paducah, Kentucky, the Tennessee River flows into the Ohio. It travels 650 miles (1,040 km) from its source near Knoxville, Tennessee, and touches seven southern states with its tributaries in the Tennessee Valley drainage area.

Floods present a major problem to Lower Mississippi towns. In the early 1900s people were sick and out of work in the Tennessee Valley. Floods leeched and scarred the soil. Homes and farms were without electricity.

In 1933 the Tennessee Valley Authority (TVA), a U.S. government agency, was established under President Franklin D. Roosevelt to relieve the problems in the area. The TVA added nine navigation locks to nine main dams on the Tennessee. They deepened and improved the channel and constructed forty-two dams on 150 miles (240 km) of tributaries. Seven state governments and private businesses improved port facilities. These improvements controlled floods, produced electric power, and increased navigation. Farmers prospered with fertile soil for their crops.

Dams on the Tennessee's tributary streams do not contain locks. They are storage dams that hold back water when there is danger of floods downstream. The Lower Mississippi is now protected from floods by flood control dams located on its major tributaries, such as the Missouri, the Ohio, and the Tennessee. Engineers receive computer-processed data hourly from rainfall and stream gauges. They decide when to hold back the floodwaters in reservoirs behind the dams, and when it is safe to release them again.

The Tennessee is one of the most completely controlled rivers in the world. The river traffic has increased more than one hundred times since 1933, as fleets of barges move down the Mississippi waterways to world markets.

What part did a barge and towboat play in man's first flight to the moon? They transported the enormous Saturn booster that lifted Astronaut Neil Armstrong's lunar capsule into space in 1969. The rocket booster was moved by water 2,200 miles (3,520 km) through the Tennessee, Ohio, and Mississippi rivers to the Gulf of Mexico and on to Cape Canaveral, Florida. The rocket, built in Huntsville, Alabama, weighed 72 tons (65.3 tonnes) and was 200 ft. (60 m) long. The barge built especially for the job was named *Palaemon* after the Greek sea god believed to protect ships.

Between Cairo, Illinois, and New Madrid, Missouri, the Mississippi channel is narrow and the banks are close. At Cairo, the Ohio crowds the muddier Mississippi against its west bank and both flow downstream. The tows are free of locks and travel faster. The Lower Mississippi widens and slows, changing shape and depth. In contrast to the rocky bluffs of the Upper Mississippi, banks are low and sometimes swampy. The river passes high land only in a few places.

From Cape Girardeau, Missouri, to Venice, Louisiana, the river is "walled in" by almost 1,900 miles (3,040 km) of levees. Floodwalls, levees, and high bluffs protect both sides of the river, with plans to extend them to 2,200 miles (3,520 km). However, because the water has to go somewhere, areas upstream and downstream flood now where they did not before.

The Corps of Engineers dredges the river and builds dikes and revetments to handle the heavy load of silt the river carries. Dikes are barriers of earth, timber, or stone about 10 or 15 feet (3 or 4.5 m) above average low water. They close off smaller channels, reduce the width of the river, and direct the flow into one main channel. They also dry up unproductive backwaters. Revetments protect the river banks from caving in and washing away. They keep the river in its course and stop its meandering. A revetment is a "mattress" of concrete and wire units. The units are assembled on a sloping deck of a launching barge or "mat" boat, which lays them in place. One of the main casting plants is located in Memphis.

Memphis sits 40 feet (12 m) above the Mississippi on the Chickasaw Bluffs at Milepost 735.0, junction of the Wolf River. The Hernando de Soto Bridge connects Arkansas and Tennessee on the Memphis waterfront close to Mud Island, a recreation and education center built by the city.

The Army Corps of Engineers lays revetments to keep the river on course and stabilize its banks.

The Memphis river port is one of the largest inland ports on the Mississippi River. It handles in excess of 14 million tons (12.7 million tonnes) of cargo annually (primarily bulk). Public River Terminals offer barge, rail, and truck services. About one third of the nation's cotton crop passes through the Port of Memphis.

Before the Civil War the shoreline was paved with cobblestones carried over on ships from England as ballast and was brought to the Mississippi by steamboat. Huge iron rings secured the hundreds of majestic vessels that docked daily. Often there would be burlap-covered bales of cotton on the cobblestone area waiting for shipment.

Memphis is the home of the blues. William Christopher Handy (1873–1958) listened to black workers loading cotton on levees as they sang made-up chants back and forth to each other. This helped them express their "blue" feelings. W. C. Handy, father of the blues, was among the first to compose blues melodies written on paper. Not far from the river, his statue overlooks Beale Street.

Elvis Presley's statue is also in Beale Street Plaza. Every year millions of visitors tour Elvis's home, Graceland.

The river inspired many sounds of music and they can all be heard at Mud Island, a 50-acre (20.25-hectare) park just offshore from downtown Memphis. Mud Island was formed by sandbars and muddy silt from the Mississippi. At the five-story River Center, a museum holds an 1870s packet boat and traces the river's history to the present day. A five-block-long River Walk winds through the middle of Mud Island. An authentic scale model shows the Lower Mississippi Valley with twenty towns beside the river's edge.

People who live and work on the Mississippi River floodplain always risk the danger of floods. In past years much of the Lower Mississippi Valley was covered with floodwaters on an average of every 2.8 years. In 200 years more than thirty serious floods were recorded. Only levees protected the river towns.

In 1927 the Mississippi overflowed its banks in the most

destructive flood in the history of the Lower Mississippi Valley. It took more than 300 lives, destroyed more than 25,000 commercial buildings and homes, and cost more than $236 million in property damage. People petitioned for federal help. A year later Congress passed the Flood Control Act of 1928. It called for improvements in levees, floodways, channels, and tributaries, and the building of more dikes, dams, and reservoirs.

In 1973, a "superflood" hit the Lower Mississippi River Valley. Guarded by a multimillion-dollar levee system, flood control structures prevented more than $7.2 million in property damage. At Cairo, where a second levee sits back 5 miles (8 km) from the first riverbank levee, the land between the two levees is a floodway or escape route, called the Birds Point–New Madrid Floodway. The Army Corps of Engineers "blew the fuse plug," a lower section of the levee, with dynamite. One fourth of the Mississippi's water passing Cairo entered the floodway and stopped the damage at Cairo. After flooding portions of land on the Missouri side, the floodwater reentered the Mississippi at a lower level at New Madrid.

In the floodplains of the Mississippi Valley, oxbow lakes are common. They are named for their U shape, resembling an ox yoke, which passes around the animal's neck. As the Mississippi meanders across its floodplain, it forms hundreds of curves, secondary channels, and U-shaped bends. As flooding increases the current speed, it moves through soft sediments and cuts new, more direct channels. Slowly the river abandons old channels, forming an "oxbow lake." If the river does not reclaim the cutoff lake, it fills in with vegetation and eventually becomes a forest.

In 1876, the nation's Centennial Year, the Mississippi River cut across one of its snakelike loops and left the harbor of Vicksburg stranded. When people looked down from the Chickasaw Bluffs, all they saw was a lake! They named the lake "Centennial."

The Army Engineers dug a 9-mile (14.5-km) canal north from Vicksburg, which diverted the Yazoo River into Lake Centennial.

The Yazoo Diversion Canal now runs past the city front at Vicksburg and empties into the Mississippi River. The canal gave Vicksburg back its harbor, and the city's economy improved.

The history of the South comes alive in Vicksburg. President Abraham Lincoln once said it was "the key to the Confederacy, and must be taken at all cost." A Civil War cannon high on a bluff overlooks the Mississippi on the site of Vicksburg National Military Park. The historic river port now ships mostly cotton surplus, lumber, livestock, and machine parts.

The busy port of Baton Rouge is located about 200 miles (320 km) downriver from Vicksburg. The port is one of the nation's largest. At night the harbor lights shimmer green, gold, and red on the water. A beacon light shines on top of the thirty-four-story Louisiana State Capitol.

At Milepost 236.0 the Baton Rouge Railway and Highway Bridge marks the upper end of Baton Rouge harbor. This is as far as the Corps has dredged for the large oceangoing ships that travel up the Mississippi. The port of Baton Rouge handles more than 73 million tons (66.2 million tonnes) of cargo annually. Many large oil refineries are located along the Baton Rouge shore. Across the Mississippi River are the great sugar plantations.

More than 100 miles (160 km) of industry stretch along the river banks between Baton Rouge and New Orleans, attracted by water power and inexpensive water transportation. This portion of the Mississippi River, called the "Industrial Corridor," holds refineries and chemical and steel plants of the major companies of the United States. The Morgan City–Port Allen Route cuts off to an Intracoastal Waterway, a canal leading to the Gulf of Mexico. At the Gulf is the entrance to the South and Southwest Passes. Ships are riding at anchor waiting for permission to enter the Mississippi.

All oceangoing vessels change pilots to come upriver. The special river pilots know the winding channels and deceiving currents. They steer ships to their destinations through one of the passes, up to New Orleans, as far as Baton Rouge.

CHAPTER SIX

THE MIGHTY RIVER

Well, I'm movin', gettin' underway
Gotta load it here,
and unload it there
Got people waitin',
Got to do my share
Well, I'm a movin'
I got materials for industry,
things for the home
Things to make life better
at work or play,
I move all night, I move all day
I'm part of the heart of the U.S.A.
Well, I'm a movin',
Yes, I'm a movin', Movin'

Song from the film
Return to the Sea
(U.S. Army Corps of Engineers)

Downriver 134 miles (214 km) from Baton Rouge is the crescent-shaped harbor of New Orleans. Popularly called the "Crescent City," New Orleans is situated 100 miles (176 km) from the mouth of the Mississippi River at the Gulf of Mexico. The modern city of New Orleans would be a floodplain if it were not for 25 to 40 feet (7.5 to 12 m) of levees around the city. It averages an annual rainfall of 57.46 inches (145.9 cm).

Connecting New Orleans with the highlands to the north is the 24-mile (38.4-km) -long Lake Pontchartrain Causeway, the longest overwater highway bridge in the world. Lake Pontchartrain is actually a bay connected to the Gulf of Mexico.

New Orleans is a city of contrasts. On the thirty-first floor of the International Trade Mart, the view overlooks the vast New Orleans port facilities. More than 5,000 ships use the wharves annually. A maritime musuem is located here with displays, ship models, and exhibits. The voices of men talking on ships in the river below can be heard over a loudspeaker.

In a city that's old yet new, a strip of skyscrapers in the central business district separates the mansions of the Garden District and the French Quarter, the *Vieux Carré* (or Old Square), the historical city section. More than 250 years ago the French explorer Jean-Baptiste Le Moyne, sieur de Bienville took his sword and scratched a rough square on the ground. There he founded *Nouvelle Orleans* (New Orleans) and named it in honor of the Duke of Orleans. Today the French Quarter exists at the site of the original town.

Buildings show the more-than-200-year influence of Creole, Spanish, and French architecture, with delightful Spanish courtyards and lacy wrought iron balconies. Every night at Preservation Hall musicians play the sounds of New Orleans Jazz, which originated in the city around the turn of the century.

Old French cemeteries contain elaborate tombs built of solid masonry placed above ground for protection from floods. In earlier years people in the New Orleans area struggled to survive floods, disease, and food shortages. The below-sea-level city has fourteen major pumping stations, one of the largest drainage systems in the world.

New Orleans has become the largest port in the United States for foreign trade and commerce. Huge seagoing freighters bring goods from foreign ports and return home with American products. It is a marketing center for the cotton, oil, salt, sulfur, natural gas, and agricultural and forest products of the area. The total shipping for the busy Port of New Orleans, including export, import, domestic, and Gulf Coast, amounts to more than 190 million tons (172.3 million tonnes) annually.

At the Port of New Orleans on the east, an Inner Harbor Navigation Canal links the Mississippi to Lake Pontchartrain. The Inner Harbor Navigation Canal also connects with an intracoastal waterway that flows into the Mississippi River Gulf Outlet, known as MR GO. Many of the wharves and complexes at the growing New Orleans port will be switched from the Mississippi to MR GO by the year 2000. The Mississippi River Gulf Outlet offers big ships a 40-mile (64-km) shorter passage to the Gulf of Mexico, as an alternate to Mississippi River entrances at South and Southwest Passes. On the west side of the river, two more intracoastal waterways cut off at Harvey and Algiers canals leading to the Gulf.

Near the 350-ft. (105-m) -high Greater New Orleans Bridge there are loading docks, fueling services, dry docks, and shipbuilding yards all along the river bend. Fleets of petroleum barges work inland as well as on the coastal waters. Small riverboat excursions sail along the marshy Louisiana bayous, territory of the legendary pirate Jean Lafitte. The Acadians (Cajuns), of French descent, live on the coastal bayous of southwest Louisiana. Exiled from Nova Scotia by the British in the middle eighteenth century, the Cajuns rebuilt their culture in Cameron Parish (County), an area of swampy flatland and shallow lakes.

In 1957 when a hurricane watch was announced for Texas and Louisiana, authorities warned residents to leave for higher ground. The Cajuns did not take the storm warning seriously. On

*In 1983 heavy rainstorms caused the Mississippi
to overflow its banks, bringing the worst floods
in twenty years to parts of Mississippi (shown here
near Vicksburg), Louisiana, and Alabama.*

June 28, 1957, a tidal wave flooded all the bayou towns. Forty thousand people lost homes and 430 died. Hurricane Audrey destroyed fishing boats, storage tanks, and oil-drilling barges. Before the Hurricane died, Audrey had blown tornadoes, flash floods, and gale winds as far north as Maine and Canada in one of the worst flood disasters in American history.

Before the river was controlled, flooding of the Mississippi was a natural occurrence. Every year the river overflowed 28,000 square miles (75,520 sq km) and withdrew its waters in a balance with nature. Today the water is confined to lower levels. It can no longer flood the alluvial valley. As a result, the river rises higher and floods are a major disaster.

A series of thunderstorms in April 1983 in the Gulf of Mexico caused the worst floods in twenty years in parts of Louisiana, Mississippi, and Alabama. At least ten people died. Oil pipelines smashed and dumped 30,000 barrels of oil into Mississippi's Homochitto River. Delta residents fought snakes and swarms of fire ants.

In New Orleans 10,000 people were without electricity or telephones. Floods forced more than 25,000 persons from their homes. The city water systems could not pump out the extra load of water. During this flood the Corps opened all 350 gates of the Bonnet Carré Spillway, 25 miles (40 km) above New Orleans.

Although hurricanes and thunderstorms can be predicted, the problems they create are enormous. Today when major flooding occurs, the Army Corps of Engineers operate under a plan called "Project Flood." It is designed to control a larger flood than the one recorded in 1927.

If a flood of this size happened, it is estimated that the amount of water coming down about 60 miles (96 km) below Natchez, at Red River landing (MP 302.4), would be 3 million cubic feet (84,950 cu m) per second. The Corps of Engineers divert half the water to the Atchafalaya River by way of the Morganza and West Atchafalaya floodways and Old River Control

Structures. The remaining half continues down the main river channel below the Morganza Floodway. The Corps sends part of this water to Lake Pontchartrain through the Bonnet Carré Spillway to the Gulf.

At the Head of Passes in the 1800s, the Mississippi River kept filling the Delta with silt, sand, and mud. The Delta is shaped like a "birdfoot" where the alluvial deposits build out at the river's mouth. The river carries 50 pounds (22.65 kg) of mud in each 1,000-cubic-foot (298-cu-m) -load of silt into the Gulf.

These sediments piled up, forming a bar that gradually obstructed the river mouth. Dredges couldn't remove the sediment fast enough to keep the channel open. Boats with a shallow draft passed at low tide, but the river wasn't deep enough for larger ships. At high tide they waited to be towed over sandbars. Dozens of wrecks hindered the channel. Citizens insisted that lawmakers do something to improve the Delta channel. New Orleans was almost cut off from commerce arriving by way of the Gulf of Mexico.

After a thirty-year study Congress asked engineer James B. Eads, builder of the St. Louis Bridge, to find a way to open up the channel. Eads proposed a system of parallel jetties 28 feet (8.4 m) deep between Southwest Pass and the Gulf of Mexico. These piers made of rock and concrete would force the river to scour out a deeper channel into the water.

In 1875 Eads was ordered to work in the south rather than the southwest passes. His task was difficult. Yellow fever plagued his workers. He had problems getting money from Congress. However, in July 1879 Eads completed a 30-foot (9-m) channel, which opened South Pass at the mouth of the Mississippi River.

In the early twentieth century the Army Corps of Engineers began the immense job of providing a jetty system for Southwest Pass. Completed in 1923, it now provides the widest channel (40 feet, 12 m) into the Mississippi River Valley for ships from the Gulf and Atlantic intracoastal waterways and foreign ports.

The Atchafalaya River in south Louisiana carves out a shorter path than the Mississippi, 150 winding miles (240 km) south to the Gulf. Mississippi River floods caused problems on the Atchafalaya and Red rivers. In 1954 Congress authorized work on Old River Control Structure, located at the confluence of the Mississippi and Atchafalaya rivers at Milepost 314.5 above Baton Rouge. A flood control plan called for navigation locks and inflow and outflow channels. Still, the possibility of the Mississippi flooding Old River Structure and flowing down the Atchafalaya Basin to the Gulf of Mexico continued to pose a real danger. After the 1973 flood the Corps built a massive rock dike to replace a fallen concrete wall and filled the underwater hole dug by the river. They redesigned the giant steel gates that control the water's flow. Presently they are constructing a $144-million auxiliary dam to be completed in 1985.

If the Mississippi River changed course, it would spill over into its tributary, the Atchafalaya River Channel. Some experts predict major damage if Old River Control Structure fails—highway and railroad bridges washed out, pipelines and oil fields shut down in the Atchafalaya Basin.

If the river bypassed Baton Rouge and New Orleans, salt water from the Gulf would invade the city ports. The Industrial Corridor of petrochemical plants, paper mills, and other factories that depend on water for production would shut down. Towns from Baton Rouge to New Orleans would lose their drinking water!

CHAPTER SEVEN

THE ABUNDANT MISSISSIPPI

I care not, I, to fish in seas,
Fresh rivers best my mind do please,
Whose sweet calm course I contemplate,
And seek in life to imitate . . .

"The Angler's Song"
Izaak Walton

The Mississippi River provides water to process materials and a river highway to transport cargo. Water flows past the western boundary of the state of Mississippi on an average of 300 to 500 billion gallons (1136 to 1893 billion liters) a day!

In 1981 the W.T. Love Hydroelectric Plant was shipped all the way from France to Louisiana. American Commercial Barge Lines moved it 1,400 miles (2,240 km) from Baton Rouge, up the Mississippi and Ohio rivers to Greenup Lock and Dam, Kentucky. It towered seven stories high and measured 192 feet (57.6 m) long by 132 feet (39.6 m) wide! A hydroelectric plant produces electricity by using the force of falling water to drive turbine generators.

Since the early 1900s, the Army Corps has been studying hydroelectric power and has become its largest builder and operator. On the Mississippi, power sites are located at St. Anthony Falls and Keokuk, Iowa. It is proposed that the next site to generate hydroelectric power be Lock and Dam 26 (Replacement).

So far it has not been practical to produce hydroelectric power at other locations because adequate elevation to produce force between water levels does not exist. Hydroelectric power does not destroy itself, and water can be used over and over; oil, coal, and gas are gone forever once they are consumed.

Water circulating around an automobile engine keeps it from overheating. In the same manner the Mississippi River supplies immense quantities of water for cooling generators at electric stations. For example, 1,000 tons (907 tonnes) of water are required for every ton of coal burned. Half the nation's electricity comes from coal. Some industrial plants require 250 to 600 tons (227 to 544 tonnes) of water per ton of steel, wood pulp, or woolen cloth.

At the Port of New Orleans, freighters and oil tankers wait at anchor to be loaded with tons of cargo arriving by barge, rail, and truck. It isn't unusual to see a 100,000-ton (90,700-tonne) freighter that holds the equivalent of 4,000 semi-trucks, 1,000 rail hopper cars, or sixty-seven barge loads of grain!

Petroleum and chemical industries prosper close to the oil fields of Louisiana, Mississippi, and Texas. Raw materials for manufacturing chemicals are found in this area. The nation's largest petrochemical company, located in Baton Rouge, manufactures over 700 products from petroleum. These products also make this area one of the most polluted on the Mississippi River.

Industrial, agricultural, and human waste change the quality of river water. Towns such as St. Paul, Rock Island, Baton Rouge, and New Orleans find their drinking water contaminated from sewage. Industrial plants emit pollutants from smokestacks. "Acid" rain occurs when rain picks up these pollutants. Raindrops turn into acid water, which destroys lake ecology, fish, and crops. Pesticides from farms are carried into streams by runoff from rainstorms. Chemical poisons seep into the soil and water and threaten human health as well as fish and wildlife.

In April 1983, four oil barges hit a St. Louis bridge, caused fires, and spilled more than 65,000 gallons (246,000 liters) of oil in the harbor. Members of the U.S. Coast Guard National Strike Force Team were sent to St. Louis to help with the cleanup. Ribbons of oil were seen as far as Cairo, Illinois. One barge sank and leaked oil from the bottom of the river bed. Oil spills upstream spread downstream. Oil globules the size of basketballs covered fish-spawning areas of the Lower Mississippi River.

An official of the Missouri Department of Natural Resources says that the high volume of water on the Lower Mississippi River dilutes chemicals so that they pose no problem to drinking water. But what happens where water flows are low in the river? And if the chemicals wash away, where will they go? We can't all live upstream.

What can be done to improve the water quality? People can decide to stop polluting the water or continue to clean it up after it's contaminated. To clean up the river, communities must enforce laws to process sewage at treatment plants before dumping in the river. All industries must recycle and treat water used in the manufacture and processing of goods. We need to strengthen laws such as the Clean Air and Clean Water Acts in order to increase control of toxic pollutants.

In 1970 Congress established the Environmental Protection Agency (EPA) to protect and improve the environment today and in the future. Among its tasks, the EPA enforces water quality standards, develops programs, and works with other agencies.

Has the EPA carried out these mandates? Over the next several years lawmakers in Congress and the people will decide the future of clean air and water.

At Morgan City, close to the mouth of the Mississippi River in the Gulf of Mexico, huge drilling rigs and oil platforms dot the shoreline. Pipelines on the sea bottom pump oil to refineries. Commercial shrimpboats haul in a day's catch. People fish and swim in the same water. Every Labor Day weekend in Morgan City, the Louisiana Shrimp and Petroleum Festival celebrates the fishing and oil industries working together.

Where the tide meets the river current at the Gulf of Mexico, it forms an estuary. The Mississippi marshes hold nutrients from the river and organisms from the sea. These two ecosystems mix together to form a rich habitat for the sea life. Nearby, ducks, herons, and egrets feed and make homes in the wetland.

The backwaters of the Mississippi River are productive ecosystems, rich with plant and animal life. Swamps, marshes, and bogs trap soil before it can enter lakes and streams. Wetlands store heavy runoff and release it slowly, reducing flood and erosion.

Every spring waterfowl fly north for the summer and in the fall migrate south for the winter. At Cairo, about 200,000 Canadian geese make their winter home at Horseshoe Lake Wildlife Refuge. Under the care of the U.S. Fish and Wildlife Service, ref-

These fish were poisoned by polluted water.
Protecting and improving the water quality
of the Mississippi is a growing concern.

uges on the Upper Mississippi River are part of the Mississippi Flyway. The river's backwaters offer homes to tens of thousands of species of plants and animals.

The Mississippi Flyway includes a series of migration routes and a refuge system. More than 400 species of birds, more than half those known in North America, fill the skies. Some travel to the Mississippi Valley from as far away as Alaska and South America. Birds help keep our vast insect and rodent population in check. In turn they provide food for other creatures. Drainage of marshes and dredging of inland waterways damage the habitats of many birds.

The Army Corps studies these problems. The organization operates its largest Waterways Experimental Station (WES) on 685 acres (277.4 hectares) in Vicksburg. Engineers check soil samples for changes in the sediment. They also test how easily soil will change and liquefy when disturbed. Liquefaction can destroy riverbank protection and threaten levee safety. Large models of dams, locks, and bridges are constructed. The Mississippi River Basin Model creates an actual flood situation and shows the aftereffects on the river basin.

Field tests by the River Studies Center at the University of Wisconsin at La Crosse show that a single barge tow passing by moves 2,700 pounds (1,215 kg) of sediment into backwaters and marshes. Fish cannot live in this muddy environment.

Across the river from La Crosse, Wisconsin, the channel for barge and other boat traffic occupies the middle of the river, with backwaters on either side. Dredge spoil near the channel was used to fill in productive wetlands.

Near Lock and Dam #7, people call a wide spot in the river Lake Onalaska, although it's really a backwater area of the Mississippi. It's fairly shallow, with an average depth of about 6 feet (1.8 m) all the way across. Lake Onalaska is quite famous for sunfish and bluegills. Fishermen park their cars at boat ramps all up and down the river. The Army Corps, the U.S. Fish and Wildlife Service, and state and local agencies keep areas open for picnicking, camping, swimming, and fishing.

Many individuals and groups of citizens share a love and concern for the Mississippi River. Each summer people celebrate the Mississippi River Revival. More than thirty-four organizations such as the Mississippi River Rats and Izaak Walton League join together in each river town. They hold festivals of music, arts, and education. Events include a flotilla of canoes and riverboats from the Headwaters at Lake Itasca to Lansing, Iowa. They celebrate the river, help clean it up, and proclaim its true meaning and value.

Sierra Club members work actively to protect rivers and national parks from toxic materials, nuclear wastes, and oil spills. They study the effects of new dams and turbulent water on fish and wildlife. The Audubon Society provides many wildlife sanctuaries across the nation. Rainey Wildlife Sanctuary, 26,800 acres (10,854 hectares) of bayou and marsh in Louisiana, is a winter feeding ground for large numbers of geese and many species of ducks.

Major problems still exist concerning the use of the Mississippi River. In 1976 Congress passed the Water Resources Development Act, which authorized funds for a four-year study by the Great River Environmental Action Team (GREAT). In five states (Minnesota, Wisconsin, Iowa, Illinois, and Missouri), work teams met with state and federal agencies. They discussed commercial navigation, water quality, fish and wildlife, placement of dredge material, and recreation. Recommendations of the GREAT studies, approved by Congress, are being carried out on the river today.

CHAPTER EIGHT

THE MAGNIFICENT RIVER

One might as well bully
the comets in their courses
and undertake to make them
behave, as try to bully
the Mississippi into right
and reasonable conduct.

Mark Twain
Life on the Mississippi

Long ago, the Indians respected the "Great Spirit" of the Mississippi as they lived beside the bountiful Big Waters. Then explorers and settlers discovered all the lands beside the powerful river and began its commerce. We learn from their experiences. Today we know the immensity of our river highway, its connecting river roads and backwaters, and we live on its floodplain.

Millions of people benefit from this valuable resource—water to drink, water for the farmers' fields, water for energy. Trucks and trains haul goods to river ports. Boats and barges deliver products along the great Mississippi, part of a far-reaching inland waterways system. Commercial fishermen take more than 25 percent of the nation's freshwater fish catch from the river. They harvest shrimp and oysters and catch catfish, crawfish, and crabs in abundance.

Recreation is a billion-dollar-plus business each year. The magnificent Mississippi is an important source of leisure-time activities. Some 230,000 acres (93,150 hectares) in the Mark Twain and the Upper Mississippi Fish and Wildlife refuges contain part of the wildest scenic beauty on the river. There is a freedom of spirit in this natural setting.

Seen from the air, the Mississippi stretches far and wide between its banks, snaking its way to the sea. A distant view of lakes, backwaters, locks, dams, dikes, and levees reveals how the river has been harnessed. Tributaries join their waters in a pilgrimage to the delta. There Ol' Man River empties its loads of silt.

At one time the river created more marshland with layers of silt and freshwater than it lost to the ocean waves. Now the Mississippi can't build the delta fast enough before it is washed away. Today Louisiana is slowly losing its vast delta land. The levees channel the river and confine the delta, protecting the citrus groves and oil refineries. The silt reaches the Continental Shelf and drops straight out to sea. How can the wetlands be restored?

Along the Gulf Coast, some 4,000 oil-drilling structures are located. The oil companies have dug out canals used for underground pipelines and floating oil rigs. These canals allow saltwater to enter freshwater marshes. Some plants and animals can't survive in the high saltwater content and lose their habitat. And rivers with too much contaminated water mean death to the animal and plant environment.

But there are some solutions. People are better able to predict the consequences of pollution today. Scientists study information from a satellite in space. The satellite reveals healthy crops on earth and spots pollutant flows into bodies of water.

The search for alternative fuels for energy goes on. There is fuel in apples, wheat, sawdust, trash—in almost anything! Energy developed and burned from different sources—the sun, the wind, the waters—is a possible answer. On the Mississippi other hydroelectric plants are proposed.

Scientists are studying the effects of carbon dioxide from fossil fuels and other organic materials. When the carbon dioxide increases in the atmosphere, the earth warms up with a "greenhouse effect." Like glass in a greenhouse, it allows the sun to pass through but does not allow the heat rays to escape. If the ground continues to warm up, the polar ice caps will melt. The seas will rise and flood the coastal areas. New Orleans and other coastal towns would be under water!

Another study concerns smoke, dust, and other solids in the atmosphere. These pollutants bring about an increase in the sun's ultraviolet rays and reflect them back into space. This loss of heat from the sun's rays could lower the earth's temperature and create a new Ice Age. If we let this happen, air and water pollution could change the earth!

A record tour of eighty-two barges went up the Mississippi yesterday. What will the river look like tomorrow? If commercial boat traffic increases, the river may look like a barge canal. If channel dredging and dam building are continued, the scenic backwaters will fill in. The habitat for fish and wildlife will be lost.

A barge on the river at sunset

If we pollute the waters, the great harvest of marine life will disappear.

The federal government has slowly been selling refuge lands for private development that threatens the future of wildlife. Today more and more people are working to protect the environment.

The Army Corps of Engineers tells us, ". . . the trend toward larger, more efficient tows will require continued improvement of the waterways. Also, increased demands for recreation will require more habor facilities for small craft and the separation of commercial and recreational traffic."

Since 1824 the U.S. government's taxpayers have invested over eight billion dollars in navigation projects and maintenance on the inland waterways. Under the present law, there is a "ton-mile" fee, a user tax of eight cents a mile, to help pay the cost. This amount will increase to ten cents in 1986.

As costly improvements are needed, the tax relieves the pressure on the federal budget to maintain the waterways. Many locks are obsolete; other new locks are proposed. However, the user charges are no small matter to barge and towing companies, commercial industries, and farm communities who ship grain from many states. The user tax raises the cost of industry and makes business less competitive at home and in world markets.

The barge and towing companies continue to move more commodities with less pollution than any other source. Some say the fee should apply to all modes of transportation, especially rail. Bills are pending in state legislatures to correct the problems.

The river requires men and women for a variety of related jobs. Research scientists are needed to study sedimentation and erosion; seismologists to measure earthquake forces; hydrologists to study water-land circulation; and biologists to study marine life.

From a small stream at Lake Itasca digging its way to a spread-out alluvial fan at the delta, the Mississippi River gathers its waters with a mighty force, a mighty power. People try to control the river for their purposes, but it will never be chained. The Mississippi will flood the banks again and again. As long as the river performs its essential role to return water to the sea, floods can never be completely prevented.

The river never sleeps. People "boat watch" the super cargo ships, paddlewheelers, tugs, trawlers, and sailboats on the Mississippi. The pink-red glow of sunset fills both sky and water. Shadows blend with the changing river current.

Perhaps you will become a Mississippi River Rat. There are many definitions. One says, "a River Rat is a person who recognizes that the Mississippi River is unique in his or her personal world and that of all whom it touches, in whatever way and for whatever reason."

INDEX